Mandir

Experience • Understand • Participate

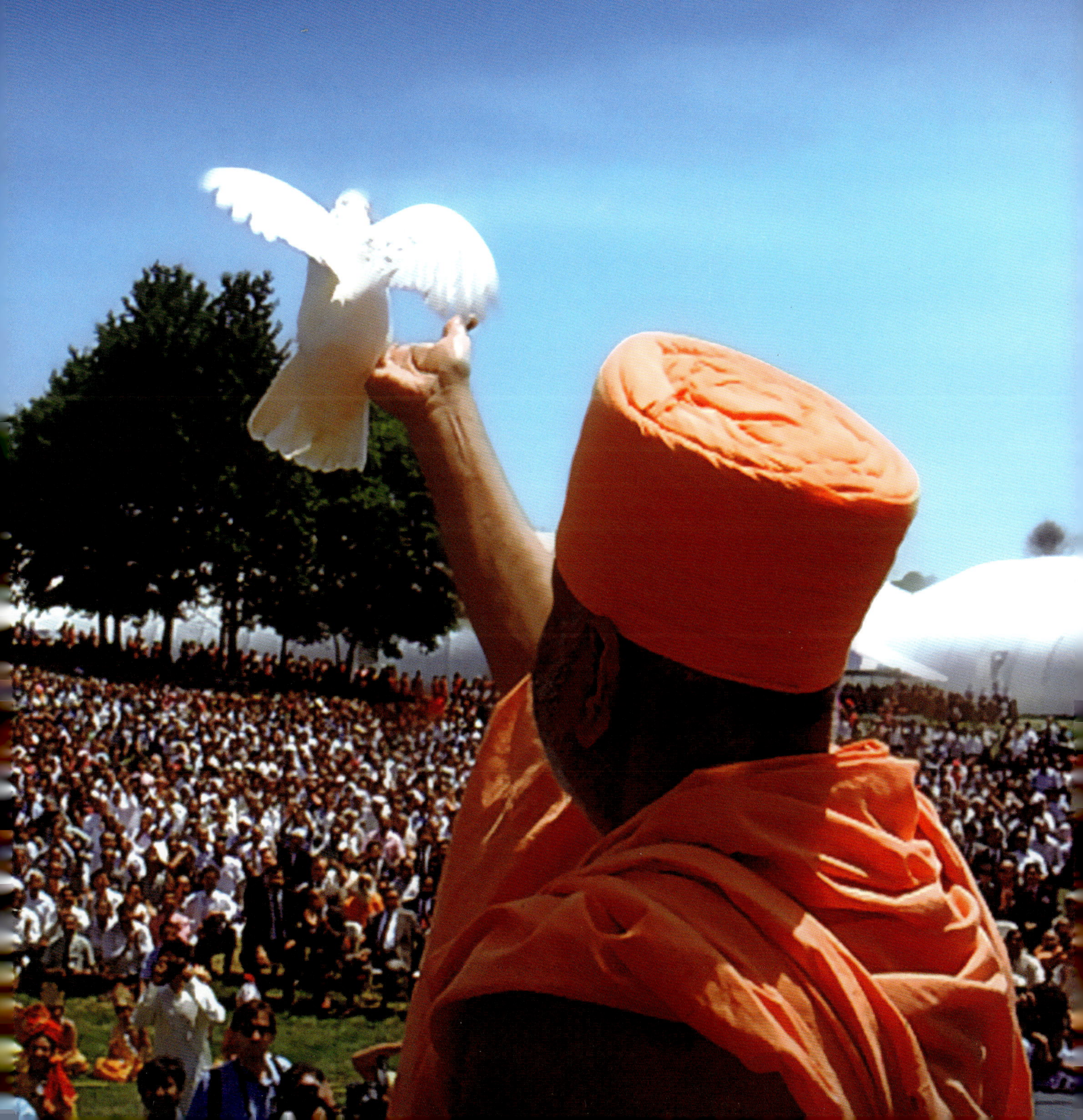

BAPS Swaminarayan Sanstha

Parabrahman, or God, manifested in northern India in 1781 and was known during his lifetime as Bhagwan Swaminarayan. In his early years, Bhagwan Swaminarayan travelled around the subcontinent and eventually settled in the western Indian region of Gujarat. There, he inspired his followers to worship God, revere the guru, and live a moral and spiritual life based on Hindu teachings.

Bhagwan Swaminarayan's third spiritual successor, Shastriji Maharaj, officially established the Bochasanwasi Shri Akshar Purushottam Swaminarayan Sanstha (BAPS Swaminarayan Sanstha) in 1907 based on principles revealed by Bhagwan Swaminarayan.

Today, the BAPS Swaminarayan Sanstha is a global, volunteer-driven Hindu organization dedicated to improving society by fostering individual spiritual growth through the ideals of faith, unity, and selfless service.

There are about 100 BAPS Swaminarayan mandirs in North America and more than 1,200 worldwide. The organization's presence in India and worldwide has been welcomed by local communities for its commitment to service, family values, and spiritual living.

Walking into a Hindu mandir for the first time and witnessing the fusion of inspiring art and architecture, ornate shrines, sacred rituals, and a serene atmosphere can be an elevating experience. This short introduction welcomes you to experience, understand, and participate while at the BAPS Shri Swaminarayan Mandir.

BAPS Shri Swaminarayan Mandir

The BAPS Shri Swaminarayan Mandir stands in continuation of a millennia-old Hindu tradition of worshipping the Divine through murtis, or sacred images, enshrined in mandirs. The Mandir is a place of:

- **Worship** – where a consistent pattern of devotional rituals, ceremonies, and practices is observed throughout the day, every day.

- **Learning** – where young and old can engage with and learn about Swaminarayan Hindu beliefs, values, and practices to kindle a spiritually uplifting and fulfilling lifestyle.

- **Celebration** – where year-round Hindu festivals allow for vibrant and joyous celebrations for the whole community.

- **Beauty** – where exquisite art and architecture are offered as a humble tribute to the inexpressible majesty and unbounded glory of the Divine.

- **Community** – where dialogue and understanding help foster greater respect, harmony, and cooperation among people of different faiths, races, ethnicities, and cultures.

- **Charity** – where the selfless spirit of volunteerism reaches out to serve the wider community and contribute meaningfully to our country.

- **Peace** - In describing a mandir, His Holiness Pramukh Swami Maharaj explains: "A mandir is a place of paramount peace, a place to realize God."

    A mandir is a place for spiritual, social, and personal development.
    This development materializes through experiences, understanding,
    and participation at mandirs.

BAPS Shri Swaminarayan Mandir
Houston, TX

BAPS Shri Swaminarayan Mandir
Atlanta, GA

BAPS Shri Swaminarayan Mandir
Robbinsville, NJ

Experience

Here, we introduce the visuals, rituals, and people you may encounter as you experience Swaminarayan Hinduism during your visit to the mandir.

1. The Architecture

Forged in the enduring spirit of reverence, adoration, and gratitude, the mandir is a humble tribute to the inexpressible majesty and unbounded glory of the Divine. As a result, the mandir is both a labor of love and a work of art. Aesthetically brilliant and technically precise, the beauty and discipline behind mandir architecture enjoys a long and celebrated history in Hinduism.

The intricately carved exterior of these traditional stone mandirs first greets the visitors, evoking feelings of purity and peace. The mandir is made of white marble, white limestone, or pink sandstone and is constructed according to the Sthapatya Shastras, the ancient treatises of Hindu architecture.[1]

BAPS Shri Swaminarayan Mandirs are carved in the Nagara style of Hindu mandir architecture. The stone used to construct the mandir was procured from India, Italy, and Bulgaria, and meticulously carved by skilled artisans in India. The stones were then shipped to the mandir site where they were assembled by traditionally-trained experts in mandir construction. Built to last a thousand years, the mandir is an inspiring legacy for the community, fostering universal spiritual values for generations to come.

Throughout the mandir, you will see carvings of liberated souls, deities, ancient sages, and exemplary devotees who are both objects of reverence and sources of spiritual inspiration.

You will also see various depictions of classical dance and music, both elements of the Hindu tradition of loving devotion to God. Additionally, carvings of auspicious animals, birds, flowers, and worship implements have been integrated into the mandir's art.

Footwear is removed upon entering a mandir in order to preserve its sanctity.

---

1. There are predominantly three types of mandirs. The shikharbaddha mandir is built of intricately carved stone with domes and shikhars, or pinnacles. The hari mandir serves a smaller congregation and uses contemporary architecture. The ghar mandir is a shrine inside a devotee's home.

BAPS Shri Swaminarayan Mandir
Chicago, IL

BAPS Shri Swaminarayan Mandir
Robbinsville, NJ

2. Mandir Components

Sthambhas - The pillars depict Hindu deities, sages, and devotees who have contributed to the richness of Hindu thought and practice. These great personalities inspire us to cultivate universal values such as honesty, empathy, non-violence, and devotion to God.

Mandovara - The exterior surrounding wall of the mandir has several tiers of ornate carvings. Each inch of stone is carved thematically, at times several inches deep, depicting stories of devotion and life.

Rupchoki - The front porch adjacent to the stairs functions as a portal to welcome the visitor into the mandir.

Chhats - Intricately carved ceilings.
Gavakshas - Ornamental windows.

Dome Ceiling

Ghummat - The majestic dome. The beautiful marble chandelier in the middle of the dome is a keystone that holds all the interlocking stone pieces together and keeps the large dome in place.

Shikhars - The pinnacles that tower into the sky, symbolizing aspiration.

Kalashes - The golden pots on top of the shikhars that signify the immortality of the soul.

Dhajas - The flags, symbolic of spiritual attainment.

BAPS Shri Swaminarayan Mandir
Toronto, Canada

BAPS Shri Swaminarayan Mandir
Houston, TX

BAPS Shri Swaminarayan Mandir
Chino Hills (Los Angeles), CA

Parabrahman
Bhagwan Swaminarayan

Aksharbrahman
Shri Gunatitanand Swami

3. Deities

Bhagwan Swaminarayan (1781 – 1830)

Parabrahman Purushottam Bhagwan Swaminarayan incarnated in northern India in 1781 to grant eternal liberation to countless souls and remove misguided religious practices.

At the age of 11, he left home and set out on a journey to inspire people to tread the spiritual path. His journey lasted 7 years, as he walked 8,000 miles over the length and breadth of the Indian subcontinent.

Heading a social and spiritual awakening, he established the Swaminarayan Sampraday at the age of 21, introducing social reforms, serving the poor and needy, and preaching against superstitions, addictions, and violence. He initiated 3,000 swamis (ordained monks) and was recognized and worshipped as Bhagwan, or God, by countless individuals during his lifetime. His teachings were compiled into the Vachanamrut, a scripture that contains the essence of the major Hindu sacred texts.

To continue his work of moral and spiritual regeneration, he promised to remain ever-present on earth through an unbroken succession of enlightened, God-realized gurus.

Gunatitanand Swami (1784 – 1867)

Gunatitanand Swami was the first spiritual successor of Bhagwan Swaminarayan.

He was revealed by Bhagwan Swaminarayan to be Akshar (or Aksharbrahman), the perfectly enlightened ideal devotee and the closest entity to God, glorified in the Vedas, Upanishads, and Bhagavad Gita.

Gunatitanand Swami extolled Bhagwan Swaminarayan's true glory as God through his profound saintliness, matchless wisdom, inspiring discourses, and constant communion with God. As Akshar, he remains manifest on earth as the enlightened guru, helping aspirants attain God-realization.

Worship of God along with his ideal devotee is an important Hindu principle that inspires us to become as pure as the ideal devotee and worship God.

Murti Puja - The practice of worshipping the sacred images of God and divine personalities is called murti puja. It helps Hindus to establish, express, and enhance their relationship with these divinities.

Hindus believe that God pervades everything and has a presence in all beings and objects. However, when an image prepared according to scriptural prescriptions is ritually infused by a spiritual authority, it becomes especially worthy of and conducive to worship.

A murti is more than a physical representation or a meditational tool. And so, devout Hindus can see beyond the stone or metal or paint, and endeavor to relate to and serve the divine spirit within.

Without the deities, the mandir would be no more than a beautiful building. With them, it becomes a sacred place of worship wherein God resides.

The main shrine is the heart of the mandir, and the murtis are its very soul. All activities of the mandir revolve around these deities, who are the focus of all forms of worship—from personal worship, like darshan, dandvats, dhyan, and mala, and daily worship, like arti, thal, and abhishek to the weekly assemblies and regular festivals throughout the year.

Due to the presence of the deities in each sacred image, they are served and attended to just like a real living sovereign. This includes their ceremonial wakening, bathing, dressing and adorning, greeting with honor during times of audience, offering of food, and resting. Trained swamis attend to the deities with a deep sense of reverence, adoration, and meditative awareness.

The Garbhagriha is the inner shrine where the murtis reside. The shrine is adorned with carved stone on the exterior, while the interior seat is made of gilded wood. The shrines appear behind carved doors, which are closed when the deities are resting, being served a meal, or being adorned.

BAPS Shri Swaminarayan Mandirs are dedicated to Bhagwan Swaminarayan, and therefore, his murti along with that of his ideal devotee, Gunatitanand Swami, is installed in the central shrine. Bhagwan Swaminarayan is also known as Purushottam, or God, and Gunatitanand Swami is also known as Akshar. Together, they are called Akshar Purushottam Maharaj. Other deities enshrined in BAPS Shri Swaminarayan Mandirs include:

Ghanshyam Maharaj

Ghanshyam Maharaj resides in the right-hand shrine. He is the childhood form of Bhagwan Swaminarayan.

Harikrishna Maharaj

The leftmost shrine houses another murti of Bhagwan Swaminarayan's childhood form, known as Harikrishna Maharaj.

Shri Krishna and Radha

Also in the leftmost shrine is the murti of Shri Krishna, an incarnation of Vishnu whose manifestation on earth is described in sacred texts such as the Mahabharat and the Shrimad Bhagavat Puran. The Bhagavad Gita, one of the most famous of Hindu scriptures, contains Shri Krishna's spiritual teachings. On the right of Shri Krishna is Radha, his ideal devotee, who exemplifies unflinching love and total dedication to God.

Shri Ram, Sita, Lakshman, and Hanuman

Shri Ram, another incarnation of Vishnu, is enshrined in the mandir together with his ideal devotee and consort, Sita, who is revered for her devotion. Shri Ram is revered for his righteousness and unfailing sense of duty to his family and the people of his kingdom. Ram's brother, Lakshman, and his devotee, Hanuman, are both revered for their selfless devotion towards Shri Ram. The story of Shri Ram, Sita, Lakshman, and Hanuman is told in the epic scripture, the Ramayan. It teaches truth, justice, valor, compassion, and other virtues.

Shri Shiv, Parvati, and Ganesh

The sacred images of Shiv, Parvati, and their son, Ganesh are also enshrined in the mandir. Shiv is portrayed here in his meditative, ascetic aspect bearing the symbols indicating his role in cosmic dissolution, which is a necessary stage in the cycle of creation. Parvati is depicted here as the ideal devotee and consort of Shiv, and embodying the related aspects of purity and power. Ganesh is revered as a remover of obstacles.

Ideal Spiritual Guru

The ideal Guru, or spiritual leader, plays a vital role in leading an aspirant to self-realization and God-realization. A lineage of gurus is central to the continued transmission and realization of spiritual knowledge by spiritual aspirants. The living Guru guides, teaches, and serves as a model for the virtues we should emulate. After Bhagwan Swaminarayan returned to his divine abode, his spiritual teachings and philosophy were continued by his spiritual successor, Gunatitanand Swami. Subsequently, the lineage of God-realized Gurus continued with Bhagatji Maharaj, Shastriji Maharaj, Yogiji Maharaj, Pramukh Swami Maharaj, and currently, Mahant Swami Maharaj.

Bhagatji Maharaj (1829 – 1897)

Bhagatji Maharaj lived a life of tremendous endeavor and unfailing faith according to the wishes of his guru, Gunatitanand Swami. His ideal moral and spiritual enlightenment singled him out as successor to Gunatitanand Swami despite his lower social status.

Shastriji Maharaj (1865 – 1951)

Shastriji Maharaj, the third spiritual successor of Bhagwan Swaminarayan, was a profound scholar of Sanskrit and Hindu scriptures. He was also an effective orator responsible for elucidating the importance of the worship of Akshar and Purushottam. Dynamic and resolute, he overcame insurmountable odds to build five grand mandirs, consecrating within them the images of Gunatitanand Swami (Akshar) and Bhagwan Swaminarayan (Purushottam). In 1907, he formally established the Bochasanwasi Shri Akshar Purushottam Swaminarayan Sanstha (BAPS).

Yogiji Maharaj (1892 – 1971)

The fourth spiritual successor of Bhagwan Swaminarayan, Yogiji Maharaj, possessed a unique personality and was a great visionary. His ever-smiling and joyous face, devotion, love, and tolerance attracted many young people. He initiated many young, learned swamis and started BAPS Youth & Children's Activities.

Pramukh Swami Maharaj (1921 – 2016)

The fifth spiritual successor in this lineage. In his efforts to serve humanity, Pramukh Swami Maharaj travelled to 52 countries, visiting 17,000 villages, cities, and towns to foster love, peace, harmony, purity, and faith within a variety of individuals—irrespective of race, class, or creed. He visited more than 250,000 homes and inspired people to live a righteous and spiritual life. He wrote over 750,000 letters resolving people's challenges and suffering. He built over 1,200 vibrant mandirs and initiated over 1,000 pious swamis.

Pramukh Swami Maharaj's entire life is an example of selfless love for humanity. His life motto, "In the joy of others, lies our own," inspired BAPS members throughout the world to engage in various services for society.

Mahant Swami Maharaj

The sixth spiritual successor and current guru in this holy lineage. He was ordained a swami by Yogiji Maharaj in 1961 and named Sadhu Keshavjivandas. As he was appointed the head (mahant) of the mandir in Mumbai, he became known as Mahant Swami. His devout, humble, and service-focused life earned him the innermost blessings of Yogiji Maharaj and Pramukh Swami Maharaj.

4. Ritual Experience

The practice of rites and rituals is intrinsic to worship at a Hindu mandir, in homes, or at the site of a significant life event. These rituals hold religious and practical significance. The following rituals are likely to be seen and experienced during a visit to the mandir:

Shringar: The shringar, or ornamenting, ritual is performed every morning prior to shringar arti. Once the deities are ritually awoken, they are adorned with colorful clothes and ornaments, and often with thematic accessories. For example, instruments may be placed around the deity to indicate an upcoming festival.

Dhyan: Dhyan, or meditation, is fundamental to stabilizing one's mind in order to concentrate on the divine form or image of God. Dhyan is also a means of experiencing the bliss of God. In the mandir, devotees perform dhyan by sitting on the floor with their legs crossed, hands on their knees, and eyes closed or focused on the murtis.

Darshan: Darshan refers to the act of beholding the deities and divine personalities with reverence and adoration. This is also extended to places and objects which have been sanctified by their holy presence.

Darshan represents one of the most fundamental forms of worship for most Hindus.

Faith and intense attachment to the divine form of God are critical components of darshan. Darshan is more than just seeing with one's eyes, but it is rather a full experience of appreciating God's glory and beauty with one's senses, mind, and soul.

Namaskar/Pranam: Hindus greet each other by bowing with folded hands or touching each other's feet as a sign of respect, while saying "Namaste" or, in the Swaminarayan tradition, "Jay Swaminarayan." This ritual also reminds the devotee to remain humble. A similar gesture of pranam is performed by devotees to the murtis.

Dandvat and Panchang Pranam: Dandavat pranam is a ritual during which male devotees offer their respect to God by lying fully prostrate on the floor with their arms stretched towards the murtis. Female devotees offer their respect to God by prostrating in a similar ritual called panchang pranam. Both are symbols of complete submission that remind devotees to surrender to God and cultivate humility.

Mala: A mala is a string of wooden beads, similar to a rosary, which devotees pass between their middle finger and thumb. Each mala consists of 108 beads, and the "Swaminarayan" mantra is chanted as each bead is turned. Devotees may choose to perform any number of malas daily. Mala jaap, or chanting the name of God, helps the devotee focus on God's divine form.

Pradakshina: Pradakshina is circumambulation, or walking clockwise around the shrine of the murti. Devotees perform pradakshina while turning the mala and chanting the Swaminarayan mantra to remind them that God is the center of their life.

Arti: The arti is one of the most visible ceremonies of the Hindu faith and features prominently at the mandir. It is a form of prayer offered in greeting and gratitude to God, reminding devotees of his presence and providence. A ceremony of light, the arti involves waving lighted wicks before the sacred images to infuse the flames with the deities' love, energy, and blessings. It is performed by swamis and pujaris (attendants to the deities) with a deep sense of reverence and adoration, while a prayer is joyously sung to the accompaniment of musical instruments, including drums, bells, gongs, and a conch shell.

After the short 5-minute prayer, the lighted wicks are passed around the congregation to allow members to receive the blessings infused within the flames. Members hover their down-turned hands over the flame and then reverently touch them to their eyes and head. More prayers and verses are sung during this time, and the whole ceremony usually takes up to 20 minutes depending on the time of day.

Thal: The living presence of the deities means that they are offered food at regular times throughout the day. These offerings are each called thal, and are a way to express devotion to God and gratitude for the food he has blessed us with.

At least three meals are offered to the deities throughout the day—breakfast in the morning (after Mangala Arti), lunch at midday (before Rajbhog Arti), and dinner in the evening (just before or after Sandhya Arti). In addition, a platter of fresh and dry fruits and fresh fruit juice is offered mid-afternoon.

Like the arti, each thal is accompanied by prayers sung to the accompaniment of musical instruments. The prayers of the thal are offered in a spirit of deep reverence, adoration and meditative awareness.

Prasad: The sanctified food that has been offered to the deities in thal is known as prasad and is distributed to devotees. In Sanskrit, 'prasad' also means grace and joy, implying that partaking of prasad is partaking of God's grace and leads to spiritual joy beyond the physical nourishment or taste provided by the food itself. Mahaprasad is the sharing of an entire meal with devotees.

Kirtan and Dhun: Kirtans are devotional songs, and dhun is the melodic recitation of the Swaminarayan mantra. Music and song are popular elements of Hindu devotional traditions. The singing of kirtans, devotional prayers, and dhun is often accompanied by musical instruments. The heart of this ritual is the remembrance of God. Devotees join in by singing and clapping. Through such participation, the devotee offers his or her devotion by extolling God's greatness.

Abhishek: Abhishek is the ancient Hindu practice of pouring water over the sacred image of God to honor him and to attain his blessings. It is also an opportunity for devotees to pray to God, asking him to cleanse one's soul. Visitors are welcome to participate in this ritual of personal devotion to the special abhishek murti of Bhagwan Swaminarayan as Nilkanth Varni or Ghanshyam Maharaj.

Chandlo: A chandlo is a mark applied on the forehead by followers of Bhagwan Swaminarayan. Different denominations within Hinduism have variations indicative of their faith. In the Swaminarayan Sampraday, males do tilak chandlo, in which the yellow, U-shaped tilak is made of sandalwood paste and represents God, and the red, round chandlo in the center of the tilak is made of vermillion powder and represents the ideal devotee. This mark symbolizes a devotee remaining in the service of God and embodies the Swaminarayan principle of devotion to God and the ideal devotee.

Celebrating Festivals: The BAPS Shri Swaminarayan Mandir is a place for quiet personal reflection as well as joyous community celebration. Festivals provide occasions to celebrate the rich Hindu cultural heritage of Hinduism, particularly through musical performances, dramas, folk dances, and art exhibits.

The Hindu calendar year is filled with festivals and days of special observances, most of which are celebrated at the mandir. Whether it be an anniversary of the Swaminarayan tradition or other festivals such as Holi, Shivaratri, Ramnavmi, Rath Yatra, Krishna Janmasthami, Diwali, or the Hindu New Year Annakut, each is celebrated with great devotion and delight.

Many of the rituals one sees in the mandir are also performed by Swaminarayan Hindus daily at their homes.

Morning Puja: Nitya Puja, or daily puja, is a prayer ritual performed every morning by Swaminarayan Hindu devotees. Puja helps an individual concentrate on the divine murtis of God and the ideal devotee. It helps to calm the mind and quiet its many thoughts. A devotee can communicate with God during daily puja and convey one's concerns and feelings directly to God.

Each morning after bathing, followers of Bhagwan Swaminarayan lay out the murtis for personal worship and meditate on God's divine form and their own atma, acknowledging that their existence transcends the body. They then engage in mental adoration and service of God, turning the mala while chanting the Swaminarayan mantra, circumambulation of the murtis, dandvat or panchang pranams, and prayer. At the end of the rituals, devotees read five verses from the Shikshapatri, a code of conduct composed by Bhagwan Swaminarayan. After finishing puja, devotees say "Jai Swaminarayan" to those present and bow, or perform panchang pranam, to their parents. Performing daily puja spiritually prepares one's mind to make the most of each day.

Ghar Mandir: Swaminarayan Hindus have a ghar mandir, or a small temple in their home, in which the sacred images of God and gurus are worshipped daily with the rituals of darshan, arti, and thal.

Ghar Sabha: Ghar Sabha is a regular gathering of family members in the home that provides a platform for spiritual development and mutual understanding. During the 15 to 30 minutes of ghar sabha, family members pray, read, and discuss spiritual and inspiring literature. They also discuss personal or family issues to foster open communication and family unity.

Understanding the Experience

The total experience at the mandir is rooted in a strong spiritual foundation. The rituals and customs one experiences at a mandir are best understood by exploring some key Hindu theological concepts.

Hinduism is one of the oldest living religions in the world. It embraces a great diversity of beliefs about God and the path to spiritual enlightenment. Though Hindus may follow different paths to attain God, the following are some core principles that are common among many Hindu traditions, including Swaminarayan Hinduism.

1. Monotheism

Though there are a variety of deities in the various shrines of the mandir, Hindu scriptures assert that there is one supreme God.

This apparent contradiction can be resolved by understanding two principles:
1) Avatarvad, or the principle of the incarnations of God, and
2) the existence of devas, or celestial beings subservient to the one supreme God.

Avatarvad - Incarnations of God

According to many Hindu scriptures, especially those of Vaishnava denominations, God manifests on earth at different times. These manifestations of God are called avatars, or incarnations of God. Hindu scriptures also explain that God manifests on the earth through his ideal devotee. Thus, the many sacred images, or murtis, in the different shrines of a mandir are of different incarnations of God and his ideal devotee.

In Swaminarayan Hinduism, Bhagwan Swaminarayan is worshipped as the Supreme God, or Parabrahman.

Devas

Hindus accept the existence of many devas, or celestial beings, who control the forces of nature and administer the universe according to God's wish.

2. Revealed Scriptures

Though there are many different schools of thought or philosophies within Hinduism, the Vedas are accepted as authoritative by Hindus. The Vedas are ancient scriptures that are direct revelations from God to the enlightened sages of ancient India. The spiritual knowledge in the Vedas is eternal. Other scriptures that have recorded the revealed words of Bhagwan Shri Krishna, such as the Shrimad Bhagavad Gita, and the teachings of Bhagwan Swaminarayan, such as the Vachanamrut, are also considered similarly authoritative.

3. Five Eternal Metaphysical Entities

Swaminarayan Hindus believe in the existence of five eternal metaphysical entities: jiva, ishvar, maya, Brahman, and Parabrahman.

The **Jiva** is the individual soul, taking birth in all life forms, including as humans. Jivas are distinct and infinite in number. Though jivas are ensnared by maya and fail to recognize their true form as distinct from the physical body, humans are privileged to have the opportunity to attain liberation from maya through the association with Brahman.

Ishvar, or celestial beings, have more powers than the jivas, but are still bound by maya. Through the powers vested in them by Brahman and Parabrahman, ishvars help to govern the forces of creation, sustenance, and destruction of the universe.

Maya is the veil of ignorance that separates the jivas and ishvars from Brahman and Parabrahman. Maya is the desire and the ignorance of the real self that hinders a spiritual aspirant's path to liberation. Maya is also Parabrahman's mystifying force through which he crafts all of creation.

Brahman is the ideal devotee of Parabrahman. Bhagwan Swaminarayan revealed Gunatitanand Swami to be Brahman and his spiritual successor. The unbroken lineage of Brahman as the guru continues for the sake of the liberation of countless spiritual aspirants. The spiritual aspirant attains Parabrahman through association with Brahman. Following the commands of the manifest form of Brahman and serving him with resolute devotion allows the spiritual aspirant to earn his grace. It is through this grace that the aspirant transcends worldly desires and becomes worthy of eternally serving Parabrahman in his divine abode, Akshardham.

Parabrahman is God, the highest existential entity. Parabrahman is sarvopari, or supreme; sarva karta, or the all-doer; pragat, or ever-present in human form; and sakar, always with a divine form.

4. Reincarnation

Punarjanma, or reincarnation, is the principle of rebirth in which the jiva progresses through the cycle of birth and death on its path to liberation. Hinduism teaches that while death may destroy the body, the jiva, or soul, is immortal—it never dies. The jiva is intrinsically pure, but because of maya—worldly desires and spiritual ignorance—it transmigrates through countless lifeforms in the cycle of birth and death. A jiva's karma, or deeds, determines its spiritual progress. A jiva's birth into a human body is the highest of all births because in the human body, the jiva has the opportunity to worship God, realize its true form to be the atman, and escape from the cycle of birth and death.

5. Liberation

Moksha, or mukti, is the liberation of the soul from maya and the cycle of birth and death. Moksha is the ultimate goal of human life. Once the devotee realizes himself to be the atman and not the body; overcomes anger, lust, greed, envy, gluttony, and other base natures; and attains God through his spiritual association with Brahman, he is able to transcend maya. The liberated jiva then resides in Akshardham, where it forever remains engaged in the bliss of God's darshan and service.

6. Karma

Karma, a word that has made its way into English vernacular, means action or deed. Karma is a law of cause and effect in which a person is cosmically accountable for his or her actions. We are constantly performing karmas whether physically or mentally. According to one's good or bad actions, God determines the consequences of one's karmas and rewards or corrects accordingly.

7. Dharma

Dharma is a moral code combined with spiritual discipline that guides one's life. Dharma is an all-inclusive term used to describe religion, the practice of righteousness, morality, and duty. Following the prescribed dharma helps one's jiva grow closer to God. Dharma is also a code of conduct that secures both worldly joys and eternal bliss.

8. Moral Disciplines

For Hindus, morality is an inseparable or integrated component of spirituality. Bhagwan Swaminarayan articulated key moral disciplines for all devotees to follow:

- Live an addiction-free life; do not consume drugs, alcohol, or tobacco.
- Eat a strict vegetarian diet, also refraining from onions and garlic.
- Refrain from stealing, violence, slander, and fraud.
- Live a morally pure life free from adultery.
- Maintain firm faith and conviction in God and guru.

9. Ahimsa (non-violence)

Ahimsa means not to hurt any creature by one's thought, speech, and actions. This principle of ahimsa is the basis for why many Hindus are vegetarians. Hindus believe that God pervades all creation; hence, each life is sacred.

10. Sadhana

The quest for the meaning and purpose of life has driven spiritual aspirants for thousands of years. Sadhana is a spiritual journey of endeavors to achieve the ultimate objective: moksha or liberation. Through sadhana, the spiritual aspirant realizes his true form to be the atma and not the physical body, thereby accelerating the journey to moksha. Bhagwan Swaminarayan showed that sadhana was striving for perfection in the practice of dharma, gnan, vairagya and bhakti.

Dharma, or righteous living, is the wisdom and self-control that enables life choices grounded in values that promote peace and harmony.

Gnan, or spiritual knowledge, is the knowledge of one's true self as the atma, or eternal soul, and that God is the all-doer and ultimate refuge.

Vairagya, or detachment, is the spiritual perspective that frees one from the constant desire for sense pleasures, enabling a spiritual connection with God.

Bhakti, or devotion, is sincere love and attachment for God, which inspires the devotee to strive to please God through his or her behavior and sentiments.

Bhagwan Swaminarayan taught that one must cultivate all four virtues to attain ultimate liberation. This integration is called ekantik bhakti, or one-pointed devotion, and its cultivation is possible through satsang.

11. The Guru

The term 'guru' is understood to mean one who dispels the darkness of spiritual ignorance. It is only through the guru that the jiva can shed the darkness of maya that surrounds it—the illusion that keeps the jiva from realizing God's greatness. The God-realized guru is Brahman incarnate. God walks, talks, and instructs through such a guru. Without the guru, a jiva cannot associate itself with God, and cannot attain moksha.

The guru has an exalted position within Hinduism. The guru is the devotee's mentor, advisor, and supporter. What qualities are exhibited by a true guru?

- A guru offers selfless love.
- A guru is free from worldly desires.
- A guru sacrifices for his devotees.
- A guru leads by example.
- A guru experiences constant oneness with God.

Pramukh Swami Maharaj was the fifth spiritual successor of Bhagwan Swaminarayan and the guru of the BAPS Swaminarayan Sanstha. His humility, faith in God, and compassion inspired millions to maintain moral and spiritual lifestyles and selflessly serve society.

He revealed his successor as Mahant Swami Maharaj, who is the sixth and current spiritual successor of Bhagwan Swaminarayan.

Weekly Satsang Assembly

Practicing Spirituality

Hinduism is a confluence of spiritual teachings and moral practices. The activities hosted at the mandir are a practical application of the faith and philosophy discussed in earlier sections of this short introduction. For a devotee, participating in the mandir's activities is instrumental in attaining moksha.

1) Satsang

Satsang is association with a true sant (a spiritual Guru), bhakta (devotee) and Bhagwan (God). It is practiced through devotion to God, the study of scriptures, and observance of dharma (code of conduct).

Satsang provides spiritual knowledge through which one develops values like patience, courage, love, and understanding in order to face the ups and downs of life with stability and peace of mind.

This same transformative power helps to free individuals from addictions and remove inner vices such as lust, ego, anger, envy, and greed.

Weekly Satsang Assembly

The key to strengthening one's Satsang is participating in the weekly satsang assembly, which is organized in every BAPS center and mandir around the world. Here, devotees come together and enjoy scriptural readings, devotional singing and chanting, and spiritual talks by learned swamis and devotees.

Along with the core Swaminarayan theological themes addressed consistently around the year, other topics regularly addressed include:

- family values • interfaith harmony and respect • education • healthy living
- caring for and respecting the elderly • dangers of substance abuse • civic engagement
- environmental responsibility • community spirit and serving the less fortunate
- channeling the energy, ideas, and potential of children and youth

Every week, there are over 11,000 weekly assemblies for men and women, youth, and teenagers, and another 7,000 weekly assemblies for children. These are held at over 1,200 BAPS Swaminarayan mandirs and 4,290 centers in India, North America, the UK, Europe, Africa, Asia Pacific, and the Middle East.

Other Satsang Activities:

- Satsang Sabha
- Satsang Shibirs (Seminars)
- Goshti (Group Discussions)
- Celebrations of Festivals
- Samuh Puja (Group Prayer)
- Cultural Programs
- Seva (Volunteer Services)

Social and Spiritual Counseling by Swamis

A swami, or Hindu monk, plays a key role in counseling within the mandir community. Swamis live a life of renunciation, dedicated to the service of God and humanity. Their spiritual experience, coupled with extensive training, prepares them to guide community members through trials on the spiritual path in everyday life.

Swamis also play a critical role in Hindu rituals. Certain swamis remain in the ritual service of the deity. Other swamis teach scriptures, sing bhajans, and counsel devotees. They dress in saffron robes and strive to live the ideals of sacrifice, detachment, and spiritual purity.

Swamis often lead various social, cultural, and humanitarian activities of BAPS. Swamis in the Swaminarayan Sampraday follow ashtanga brahmacharya, or eight-fold celibacy. This vow of strict self-discipline is intended to facilitate complete immersion in devotion and in the single-minded service of God, his devotees, and society at large.

2) Cultural, Recreational, and Educational Experiences

In addition to spiritual growth, a mandir gifts the community with a platform to develop culturally and educationally. In support of this effort, the mandir complex includes a variety of facilities to host activities that craft these cultural, recreational, and educational experiences.

Children & Youth Development

The true prosperity of the world lies in its children and youth. The values we instill in our children and youth today will allow them to mold their lives to become balanced, responsible, and contributing members of society. BAPS promotes personal development of our children and youth through an emphasis on spiritual, family, and cultural activities such as:

- Children's Sabha (Spiritual Assemblies) • On-campus Meetings for College Students
- Music Classes • Language Classes • Art Classes • Cooking Classes
- Celebration of Festivals • Parent Awareness Forums
- Folk Dances and Musical Performances • Educational Awareness and Tutoring
- SAT Classes • Career Fairs • "Experience India" Trips • Yoga Classes • Walkathons
- Athletic Events and Tournaments • Outings and Educational Retreats • Conventions

Coexistence & Harmony

Stemming from the belief that there can be unity in diversity, BAPS values living in harmony with others. Worshippers and visitors of all cultures, beliefs, and backgrounds are welcomed with warmth and respect at all BAPS mandirs.

BAPS members, young and old, live harmoniously with their neighbors and proactively contribute to their community through a variety of activities.

Believing that dialogue among societal and spiritual leaders is essential for peaceful coexistence, Pramukh Swami Maharaj has worked to foster communication with leaders of other religious groups and governments. This effort has also led to leaders and members of BAPS participating in various inter-faith conferences and programs.

3) Seva – Contributing to Society

Hinduism emphasizes the importance of seva, which is to selflessly serve both God and humanity. The concept of seva is associated with love, tolerance, and humility. Seva is not just community service, volunteer work, or donating money; rather, it is cultivating a mindset that puts others before one's self, and sacrificing and serving with devotion. Hindus believe that the opportunity to serve God, guru, and the community is a great privilege. Thus, all acts of seva are completed with a sense of joy.

Mandirs play a critical role in supporting the humanitarian initiatives of BAPS in conjunction with its humanitarian services arm, BAPS Charities. In addition to the financial support provided to many local and national community projects through fundraising efforts such as Walkathons, the organization harnesses the efforts and collective spirit of volunteers around the world to serve individuals, families, and communities.

Highlights of Global Service Activities

Environmental Activities

- Thousands of tons of paper collected for recycling annually
- Water conservation projects in hundreds of villages in India
- Environmental-friendly construction of mandirs, including preserving green spaces, planting thousands of trees and shrubs, and minimizing the carbon footprint of the mandir foundation
- 2016 to 2019: 361,000 trees planted in partnership with The Nature Conservancy (TNC)

Health & Wellness

- Seven charitable hospitals and healthcare clinics in India, treating over 500,000 patients annually
- Since 1999, 14 mobile medical clinics have treated 3.9 million impoverished villagers in India free of charge
- Over 140 Medico-spiritual conferences have enlightened over 40,000 doctors
- Over 2 million people inspired to quit addictions
- In North America, since 2010, 468 diagnostic health fairs, benefiting over 110,000 participants
- Annual blood donation drives in North America have helped save over 44,000 lives since 2006
- Bone marrow drives, Children's health and safety days, and many other activities

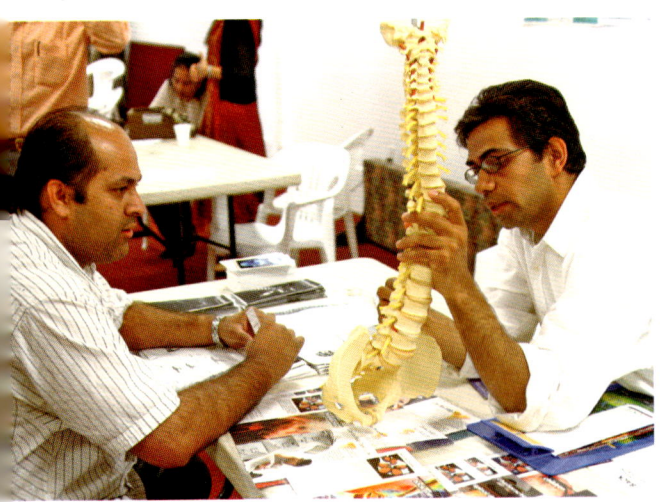

Educational Services

- In India, 24 schools and hostels provide over 12,000 students with value-based education annually
- 55 schools built in disaster-hit areas in India
- Over 5,000 scholarships awarded annually

Humanitarian Services

Over 40 disaster relief operations successfully managed, reaching out during times of urgent need, first to assist and then to empower people to return to their normal lives. BAPS has been there to provide immediate food and medical aid, permanent rehabilitation, and long-term socio-economic assistance.

- More than 1,800,000 hot meals served and 4,190 homes constructed in the 2001 earthquake in Gujarat
- 530 volunteers served hot meals to victims of Hurricanes Katrina and Rita in 2005
- Founding Sponsor of the 9/11 Memorial & Museum in New York
- 2010 - Haiti Earthquake Relief - Partnered with UNICEF and donated $63,678
- 2013 - Philippines Typhoon Haiyan Relief – Partnered with UNICEF and donated $11,000
- 2014 - Uttarakhand Flood Relief - $65,000 donated for relief
- 2015 - Nepal Earthquake Relief - $30,000 to UNICEF, $30,000 to World Food Program, $25,000 to One Heart Worldwide, $25,000 to Embassy of Nepal, $25,000 to Direct Relief
- 2016 - Fort McMurray, Canada wildfire relief efforts - 300 hot meals / 100 evacuees offered shelter / 108 bedroom sets
- 2017 - Hurricane Harvey relief Efforts - 100 volunteers / 8,000 volunteer hours / 4,500 hot meals / 3,000 drywall sheets for rebuilding homes
- 2018 - California wildfires relief - $35,000 donated
- 2019 - California wildfires relief - $25,000 donated

Volunteers

- Over 55,000 volunteers worldwide
- Over 5,000,000 hours of service annually
- Globally networked in 3,850 centers

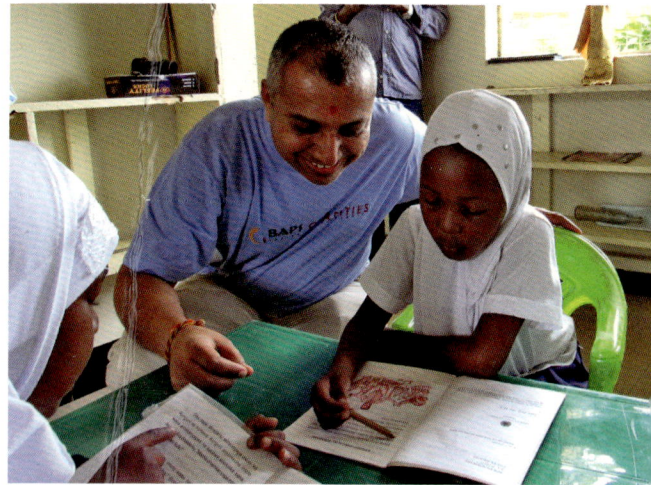
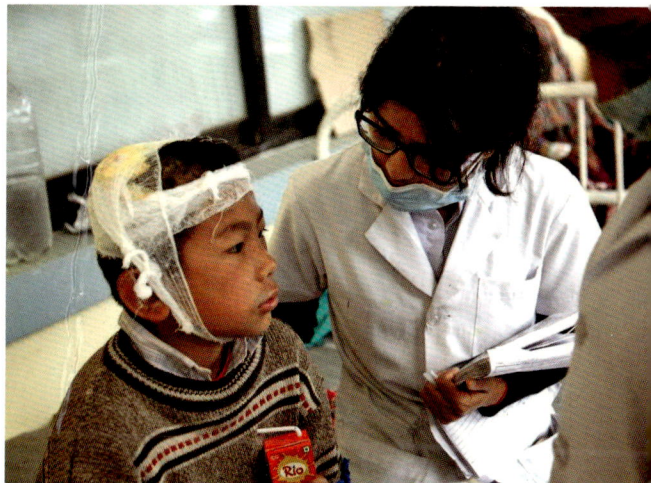

"My heart running here and there, settles in His presence, in His home.
My mind at peace; my thoughts silent.
My limbs engaged in service; my breath singing His song, His glory.
Surdas's eyes caught gazing at His splendid form; my soul one with His—here,
He speaks, listens, and responds."

- Surdas, 16th century North Indian bhakti poet

Visit us on the web for directions, updated darshan timings, and upcoming events.

BAPS.org/Atlanta • BAPS.org/Chicago • BAPS.org/Houston • BAPS.org/LosAngeles
BAPS.org/Robbinsville • BAPS.org/Toronto

For more information on BAPS's global presence, youth activities, publications, vegetarian food and dietary products, and humanitarian efforts, please visit us on the web:

www.kids.BAPS.org • www.Aksharpith.BAPS.org
www.Shayona.BAPS.org • www.BAPScharities.org

www.BAPS.org

Mandir: Experience | Understand | Participate

SKU 14761   USD $1.00   CAD $1.25

Brahmaswarup
Pramukh Swami Maharaj

Pragat Brahmaswarup
Mahant Swami Maharaj

BAPS Swaminarayan Sanstha® | www.BAPS.org

ISBN 9781947461000